THE ANTS GO MARCHING

Illustrated by Jeffrey Scherer

SCHOLASTIC INC. Cartwheel B·O·O·K·S®

New York   Toronto   London   Auckland   Sydney
Mexico City   New Delhi   Hong Kong   Buenos Aires

To my sisters, a couple of ants,
Susan and Nancy
—J.S.

ISBN 0-439-75560-3

Copyright © 2002 by Scholastic Inc.
Illustrations copyright © 2002 by Jeffrey Scherer.
All rights reserved. Published by Scholastic Inc.
SCHOLASTIC, CARTWHEEL BOOKS, SING AND READ STORYBOOK, and associated logos
are trademarks and/or registered trademarks of Scholastic Inc.

12 11 10 9 8 7 6 5 4 3 2 1   5 6 7 8 9/0

Printed in the U.S.A. 23 • First printing, April 2002
This edition first printing, September 2005

The ants go marching one by one.
Hurrah! Hurrah!
The ants go marching one by one.
Hurrah! Hurrah!

The ants go marching one by one,
the little one stops to suck his thumb,
and they all go marching
down to the ground
to get out of the rain.
BOOM! BOOM! BOOM!

The ants go marching two by two.
Hurrah! Hurrah!
The ants go marching two by two.
Hurrah! Hurrah!
The ants go marching two by two,
the little one stops to tie his shoe,
and they all go marching
down to the ground
to get out of the rain.
BOOM! BOOM! BOOM!

The ants go marching three by three.
Hurrah! Hurrah!
The ants go marching three by three.
Hurrah! Hurrah!

The ants go marching three by three,
the little one stops to ride a bee,
and they all go marching
down to the ground
to get out of the rain.
BOOM! BOOM! BOOM!

The ants go marching four by four.
Hurrah! Hurrah!
The ants go marching four by four.
Hurrah! Hurrah!
The ants go marching four by four,
the little one stops to shut the door,
and they all go marching
down to the ground
to get out of the rain.
BOOM! BOOM! BOOM!

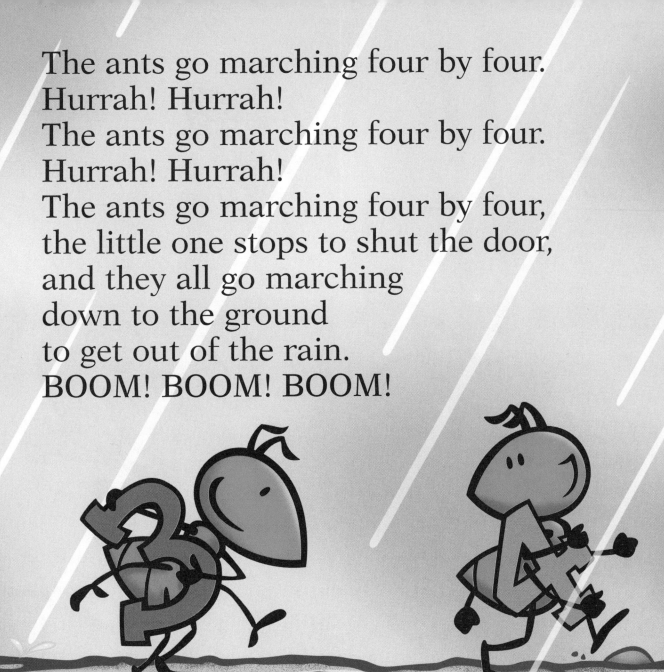

The ants go marching five by five.
Hurrah! Hurrah!
The ants go marching five by five.
Hurrah! Hurrah!

The ants go marching five by five,
the little one stops to jump and jive,
and they all go marching
down to the ground
to get out of the rain.
BOOM! BOOM! BOOM!

The ants go marching six by six.
Hurrah! Hurrah!
The ants go marching six by six.
Hurrah! Hurrah!

The ants go marching six by six,
the little one stops to pick up sticks,
and they all go marching
down to the ground
to get out of the rain.
BOOM! BOOM! BOOM!

The ants go marching seven by seven.
Hurrah! Hurrah!
The ants go marching seven by seven.
Hurrah! Hurrah!

The ants go marching seven by seven,
the little one stops to write with a pen,
and they all go marching
down to the ground
to get out of the rain.
BOOM! BOOM! BOOM!

The ants go marching eight by eight.
Hurrah! Hurrah!
The ants go marching eight by eight.
Hurrah! Hurrah!
The ants go marching eight by eight,
the little one stops to roller-skate,
and they all go marching
down to the ground
to get out of the rain.
BOOM! BOOM! BOOM!

The ants go marching nine by nine.
Hurrah! Hurrah!
The ants go marching nine by nine.
Hurrah! Hurrah!

The ants go marching nine by nine,
the little one stops to drink and dine,
and they all go marching
down to the ground
to get out of the rain.
BOOM! BOOM! BOOM!

The ants go marching ten by ten.
Hurrah! Hurrah!
The ants go marching ten by ten.
Hurrah! Hurrah!
The ants go marching ten by ten,
the little one stops to say, "THE END!"
And they all go marching
down to the ground
to get out of the rain.
BOOM! BOOM! BOOM!

The ants go march - ing one by one. Hur-

rah! _____ Hur - rah! _____ The

ants go march - ing one by one. Hur-

rah! _____ Hur - rah! _____ The

ants go march - ing one by one, the

lit - tle one stops to suck his thumb, and they

all go march - ing

down to the ground to get

out of the rain. BOOM! BOOM! BOOM!